DIGITAL PASSWOF

"Internet Password Logbook To Prote
In One Easy & Orgai..

THIS BOOK BELONGS TO

____

____

____

SOFTWARE INFORMATION

Software: ___________________________

Purchase Date: ___________________________

License Key: ___________________________

____

Software: ___________________________

Purchase Date: ___________________________

License Key: ___________________________

____

Software: ___________________________

Purchase Date: ___________________________

License Key: ___________________________

____

Software: ___________________________

Purchase Date: ___________________________

License Key: ___________________________

____

Software: ___________________________

Purchase Date: ___________________________

License Key: ___________________________

____

COMPUTER INFORMATION

Computer #1: _______________

Model: _______________

Serial Number: _______________

Purchase Date: _______________

Warranty: _______________

Support: _______________

Notes: _______________

Computer #2: _______________

Model: _______________

Serial Number: _______________

Purchase Date: _______________

Warranty: _______________

Support: _______________

Notes: _______________

Computer #3: _______________

Model: _______________

Serial Number: _______________

Purchase Date: _______________

Warranty: _______________

Support: _______________

Notes: _______________

NETWORK INFORMATION #1

ISP Name:

Website:

Account Number:

Email:

Password:

Support:

Notes:

Modem/Router:

Model:

Serial Number:

Admin URL:

Username:

Password:

Notes:

SSID (WiFi Network Name):

Password:

Security Mode:

Notes:

NETWORK INFORMATION #2

ISP Name: _______________________

Website: _______________________

Account Number: _______________________

Email: _______________________

Password: _______________________

Support: _______________________

Notes: _______________________

____

Modem/Router: _______________________

Model: _______________________

Serial Number: _______________________

Admin URL: _______________________

Username: _______________________

Password: _______________________

Notes: _______________________

____

SSID (WiFi Network Name): _______________________

Password: _______________________

Security Mode: _______________________

Notes: _______________________

____

Website:

Email:

Username:

Date/Password:

Date/Password:

Date/Password:

Notes:

Website:

Email:

Username:

Date/Password:

Date/Password:

Date/Password:

Notes:

Website:

Email:

Username:

Date/Password:

Date/Password:

Date/Password:

Notes:

A

Website:

Email:

Username:

Date/Password:

Date/Password:

Date/Password:

Notes:

Website:

Email:

Username:

Date/Password:

Date/Password:

Date/Password:

Notes:

Website:

Email:

Username:

Date/Password:

Date/Password:

Date/Password:

Notes:

Website:

Email:

Username:

Date/Password:

Date/Password:

Date/Password:

Notes:

Website:

Email:

Username:

Date/Password:

Date/Password:

Date/Password:

Notes:

Website:

Email:

Username:

Date/Password:

Date/Password:

Date/Password:

Notes:

Website:

Email:

Username:

Date/Password:

Date/Password:

Date/Password:

Notes:

Website:

Email:

Username:

Date/Password:

Date/Password:

Date/Password:

Notes:

Website:

Email:

Username:

Date/Password:

Date/Password:

Date/Password:

Notes:

Website:
Email:
Username:
Date/Password:
Date/Password:
Date/Password:
Notes:

Website:
Email:
Username:
Date/Password:
Date/Password:
Date/Password:
Notes:

Website:
Email:
Username:
Date/Password:
Date/Password:
Date/Password:
Notes:

Website:

Email:

Username:

Date/Password:

Date/Password:

Date/Password:

Notes:

Website:

Email:

Username:

Date/Password:

Date/Password:

Date/Password:

Notes:

Website:

Email:

Username:

Date/Password:

Date/Password:

Date/Password:

Notes:

Website: ___________________________
Email: _____________________________
Username: __________________________
Date/Password: _____________________
Date/Password: _____________________
Date/Password: _____________________
Notes: _____________________________
____

Website: ___________________________
Email: _____________________________
Username: __________________________
Date/Password: _____________________
Date/Password: _____________________
Date/Password: _____________________
Notes: _____________________________
____

Website: ___________________________
Email: _____________________________
Username: __________________________
Date/Password: _____________________
Date/Password: _____________________
Date/Password: _____________________
Notes: _____________________________
____

Website:

Email:

Username:

Date/Password:

Date/Password:

Date/Password:

Notes:

Website:

Email:

Username:

Date/Password:

Date/Password:

Date/Password:

Notes:

Website:

Email:

Username:

Date/Password:

Date/Password:

Date/Password:

Notes:

C

Website:

Email:

Username:

Date/Password:

Date/Password:

Date/Password:

Notes:

Website:

Email:

Username:

Date/Password:

Date/Password:

Date/Password:

Notes:

Website:

Email:

Username:

Date/Password:

Date/Password:

Date/Password:

Notes:

Website:

Email:

Username:

Date/Password:

Date/Password:

Date/Password:

Notes:

Website:

Email:

Username:

Date/Password:

Date/Password:

Date/Password:

Notes:

Website:

Email:

Username:

Date/Password:

Date/Password:

Date/Password:

Notes:

Website: _______________________
Email: _______________________
Username: _______________________
Date/Password: _______________________
Date/Password: _______________________
Date/Password: _______________________
Notes: _______________________
____

Website: _______________________
Email: _______________________
Username: _______________________
Date/Password: _______________________
Date/Password: _______________________
Date/Password: _______________________
Notes: _______________________
____

Website: _______________________
Email: _______________________
Username: _______________________
Date/Password: _______________________
Date/Password: _______________________
Date/Password: _______________________
Notes: _______________________
____

Website:

Email:

Username:

Date/Password:

Date/Password:

Date/Password:

Notes:

Website:

Email:

Username:

Date/Password:

Date/Password:

Date/Password:

Notes:

Website:

Email:

Username:

Date/Password:

Date/Password:

Date/Password:

Notes:

D

Website: ____

Email: ____

Username: ____

Date/Password: ____

Date/Password: ____

Date/Password: ____

Notes: ____

____

Website: ____

Email: ____

Username: ____

Date/Password: ____

Date/Password: ____

Date/Password: ____

Notes: ____

____

Website: ____

Email: ____

Username: ____

Date/Password: ____

Date/Password: ____

Date/Password: ____

Notes: ____

____

Website:

Email:

Username:

Date/Password:

Date/Password:

Date/Password:

Notes:

Website:

Email:

Username:

Date/Password:

Date/Password:

Date/Password:

Notes:

Website:

Email:

Username:

Date/Password:

Date/Password:

Date/Password:

Notes:

Website:
Email:
Username:
Date/Password:
Date/Password:
Date/Password:
Notes:

Website:
Email:
Username:
Date/Password:
Date/Password:
Date/Password:
Notes:

Website:
Email:
Username:
Date/Password:
Date/Password:
Date/Password:
Notes:

Website: _______________________________

Email: _______________________________

Username: _______________________________

Date/Password: _______________________________

Date/Password: _______________________________

Date/Password: _______________________________

Notes: _______________________________

____

D

Website: _______________________________

Email: _______________________________

Username: _______________________________

Date/Password: _______________________________

Date/Password: _______________________________

Date/Password: _______________________________

Notes: _______________________________

____

Website: _______________________________

Email: _______________________________

Username: _______________________________

Date/Password: _______________________________

Date/Password: _______________________________

Date/Password: _______________________________

Notes: _______________________________

____

Website: ____

Email: ____

Username: ____

Date/Password: ____

Date/Password: ____

Date/Password: ____

Notes: ____

____

Website: ____

Email: ____

Username: ____

Date/Password: ____

Date/Password: ____

Date/Password: ____

Notes: ____

____

Website: ____

Email: ____

Username: ____

Date/Password: ____

Date/Password: ____

Date/Password: ____

Notes: ____

____

Website:

Email:

Username:

Date/Password:

Date/Password:

Date/Password:

Notes:

Website:

Email:

Username:

Date/Password:

Date/Password:

Date/Password:

Notes:

Website:

Email:

Username:

Date/Password:

Date/Password:

Date/Password:

Notes:

Website:
Email:
Username:
Date/Password:
Date/Password:
Date/Password:
Notes:

Website:
Email:
Username:
Date/Password:
Date/Password:
Date/Password:
Notes:

Website:
Email:
Username:
Date/Password:
Date/Password:
Date/Password:
Notes:

Website:____

Email:____

Username:____

Date/Password:____

Date/Password:____

Date/Password:____

Notes:____

____

Website:____

Email:____

Username:____

Date/Password:____

Date/Password:____

Date/Password:____

Notes:____

____

Website:____

Email:____

Username:____

Date/Password:____

Date/Password:____

Date/Password:____

Notes:____

____

F

Website:

Email:

Username:

Date/Password:

Date/Password:

Date/Password:

Notes:

Website:

Email:

Username:

Date/Password:

Date/Password:

Date/Password:

Notes:

Website:

Email:

Username:

Date/Password:

Date/Password:

Date/Password:

Notes:

Website:

Email:

Username:

Date/Password:

Date/Password:

Date/Password:

Notes:

Website:

Email:

Username:

Date/Password:

Date/Password:

Date/Password:

Notes:

Website:

Email:

Username:

Date/Password:

Date/Password:

Date/Password:

Notes:

Website:
Email:
Username:
Date/Password:
Date/Password:
Date/Password:
Notes:

Website:
Email:
Username:
Date/Password:
Date/Password:
Date/Password:
Notes:

Website:
Email:
Username:
Date/Password:
Date/Password:
Date/Password:
Notes:

Website:

Email:

Username:

Date/Password:

Date/Password:

Date/Password:

Notes:

Website:

Email:

Username:

Date/Password:

Date/Password:

Date/Password:

Notes:

Website:

Email:

Username:

Date/Password:

Date/Password:

Date/Password:

Notes:

G

Website:

Email:

Username:

Date/Password:

Date/Password:

Date/Password:

Notes:

Website:

Email:

Username:

Date/Password:

Date/Password:

Date/Password:

Notes:

Website:

Email:

Username:

Date/Password:

Date/Password:

Date/Password:

Notes:

Website:

Email:

Username:

Date/Password:

Date/Password:

Date/Password:

Notes:

G

Website:

Email:

Username:

Date/Password:

Date/Password:

Date/Password:

Notes:

Website:

Email:

Username:

Date/Password:

Date/Password:

Date/Password:

Notes:

G

Website:

Email:

Username:

Date/Password:

Date/Password:

Date/Password:

Notes:

Website:

Email:

Username:

Date/Password:

Date/Password:

Date/Password:

Notes:

Website:

Email:

Username:

Date/Password:

Date/Password:

Date/Password:

Notes:

Website:

Email:

Username:

Date/Password:

Date/Password:

Date/Password:

Notes:

G

Website:

Email:

Username:

Date/Password:

Date/Password:

Date/Password:

Notes:

Website:

Email:

Username:

Date/Password:

Date/Password:

Date/Password:

Notes:

Website:

Email:

Username:

Date/Password:

Date/Password:

Date/Password:

Notes:

Website:

Email:

Username:

Date/Password:

Date/Password:

Date/Password:

Notes:

Website:

Email:

Username:

Date/Password:

Date/Password:

Date/Password:

Notes:

Website:

Email:

Username:

Date/Password:

Date/Password:

Date/Password:

Notes:

Website:

Email:

Username:

Date/Password:

Date/Password:

Date/Password:

Notes:

Website:

Email:

Username:

Date/Password:

Date/Password:

Date/Password:

Notes:

Website:

Email:

Username:

Date/Password:

Date/Password:

Date/Password:

Notes:

Website:

Email:

Username:

Date/Password:

Date/Password:

Date/Password:

Notes:

Website:

Email:

Username:

Date/Password:

Date/Password:

Date/Password:

Notes:

Website: _______________________________

Email: _______________________________

Username: _______________________________

Date/Password: _______________________________

Date/Password: _______________________________

Date/Password: _______________________________

Notes: _______________________________

____

Website: _______________________________

Email: _______________________________

Username: _______________________________

Date/Password: _______________________________

Date/Password: _______________________________

Date/Password: _______________________________

Notes: _______________________________

____

Website: _______________________________

Email: _______________________________

Username: _______________________________

Date/Password: _______________________________

Date/Password: _______________________________

Date/Password: _______________________________

Notes: _______________________________

____

Website:

Email:

Username:

Date/Password:

Date/Password:

Date/Password:

Notes:

Website:

Email:

Username:

Date/Password:

Date/Password:

Date/Password:

Notes:

Website:

Email:

Username:

Date/Password:

Date/Password:

Date/Password:

Notes:

Website:

Email:

Username:

Date/Password:

Date/Password:

Date/Password:

Notes:

Website:

Email:

Username:

Date/Password:

Date/Password:

Date/Password:

Notes:

Website:

Email:

Username:

Date/Password:

Date/Password:

Date/Password:

Notes:

Website:

Email:

Username:

Date/Password:

Date/Password:

Date/Password:

Notes:

Website:

Email:

Username:

Date/Password:

Date/Password:

Date/Password:

Notes:

Website:

Email:

Username:

Date/Password:

Date/Password:

Date/Password:

Notes:

Website:_______________________________________

Email:____

Username:______________________________________

Date/Password:_________________________________

Date/Password:_________________________________

Date/Password:_________________________________

Notes:____

____

Website:_______________________________________

Email:____

Username:______________________________________

Date/Password:_________________________________

Date/Password:_________________________________

Date/Password:_________________________________

Notes:____

____

Website:_______________________________________

Email:____

Username:______________________________________

Date/Password:_________________________________

Date/Password:_________________________________

Date/Password:_________________________________

Notes:____

____

J

Website:

Email:

Username:

Date/Password:

Date/Password:

Date/Password:

Notes:

Website:

Email:

Username:

Date/Password:

Date/Password:

Date/Password:

Notes:

Website:

Email:

Username:

Date/Password:

Date/Password:

Date/Password:

Notes:

Website:

Email:

Username:

Date/Password:

Date/Password:

Date/Password:

Notes:

Website:

Email:

Username:

Date/Password:

Date/Password:

Date/Password:

Notes:

Website:

Email:

Username:

Date/Password:

Date/Password:

Date/Password:

Notes:

J

Website:

Email:

Username:

Date/Password:

Date/Password:

Date/Password:

Notes:

Website:

Email:

Username:

Date/Password:

Date/Password:

Date/Password:

Notes:

Website:

Email:

Username:

Date/Password:

Date/Password:

Date/Password:

Notes:

Website: _______________________________

Email: _______________________________

Username: _______________________________

Date/Password: _______________________________

Date/Password: _______________________________

Date/Password: _______________________________

Notes: _______________________________

____

Website: _______________________________

Email: _______________________________

Username: _______________________________

Date/Password: _______________________________

Date/Password: _______________________________

Date/Password: _______________________________

Notes: _______________________________

____

J

Website: _______________________________

Email: _______________________________

Username: _______________________________

Date/Password: _______________________________

Date/Password: _______________________________

Date/Password: _______________________________

Notes: _______________________________

____

Website:

Email:

Username:

Date/Password:

Date/Password:

Date/Password:

Notes:

Website:

Email:

Username:

Date/Password:

Date/Password:

Date/Password:

Notes:

Website:

Email:

Username:

Date/Password:

Date/Password:

Date/Password:

Notes:

Website:

Email:

Username:

Date/Password:

Date/Password:

Date/Password:

Notes:

Website:

Email:

Username:

Date/Password:

Date/Password:

Date/Password:

Notes:

Website:

Email:

Username:

Date/Password:

Date/Password:

Date/Password:

Notes:

A
B
C
D
E
F
G
H
I
J
K
L
M
N
O
P
Q
R
S
T
U
V
W
X
Y
Z

Website: ____

Email: ____

Username: ____

Date/Password: ____

Date/Password: ____

Date/Password: ____

Notes: ____

____

Website: ____

Email: ____

Username: ____

Date/Password: ____

Date/Password: ____

Date/Password: ____

Notes: ____

____

Website: ____

Email: ____

Username: ____

Date/Password: ____

Date/Password: ____

Date/Password: ____

Notes: ____

____

Website:

Email:

Username:

Date/Password:

Date/Password:

Date/Password:

Notes:

Website:

Email:

Username:

Date/Password:

Date/Password:

Date/Password:

Notes:

Website:

Email:

Username:

Date/Password:

Date/Password:

Date/Password:

Notes:

Website: _______________________________

Email: _______________________________

Username: _______________________________

Date/Password: _______________________________

Date/Password: _______________________________

Date/Password: _______________________________

Notes: _______________________________

____

Website: _______________________________

Email: _______________________________

Username: _______________________________

Date/Password: _______________________________

Date/Password: _______________________________

Date/Password: _______________________________

Notes: _______________________________

____

Website: _______________________________

Email: _______________________________

Username: _______________________________

Date/Password: _______________________________

Date/Password: _______________________________

Date/Password: _______________________________

Notes: _______________________________

____

Website:

Email:

Username:

Date/Password:

Date/Password:

Date/Password:

Notes:

Website:

Email:

Username:

Date/Password:

Date/Password:

Date/Password:

Notes:

Website:

Email:

Username:

Date/Password:

Date/Password:

Date/Password:

Notes:

Website:

Email:

Username:

Date/Password:

Date/Password:

Date/Password:

Notes:

Website:

Email:

Username:

Date/Password:

Date/Password:

Date/Password:

Notes:

Website:

Email:

Username:

Date/Password:

Date/Password:

Date/Password:

Notes:

Website:

Email:

Username:

Date/Password:

Date/Password:

Date/Password:

Notes:

Website:

Email:

Username:

Date/Password:

Date/Password:

Date/Password:

Notes:

Website:

Email:

Username:

Date/Password:

Date/Password:

Date/Password:

Notes:

Website:

Email:

Username:

Date/Password:

Date/Password:

Date/Password:

Notes:

Website:

Email:

Username:

Date/Password:

Date/Password:

Date/Password:

Notes:

Website:

Email:

Username:

Date/Password:

Date/Password:

Date/Password:

Notes:

Website:

Email:

Username:

Date/Password:

Date/Password:

Date/Password:

Notes:

Website:

Email:

Username:

Date/Password:

Date/Password:

Date/Password:

Notes:

Website:

Email:

Username:

Date/Password:

Date/Password:

Date/Password:

Notes:

M

Website:

Email:

Username:

Date/Password:

Date/Password:

Date/Password:

Notes:

Website:

Email:

Username:

Date/Password:

Date/Password:

Date/Password:

Notes:

Website:

Email:

Username:

Date/Password:

Date/Password:

Date/Password:

Notes:

Website:

Email:

Username:

Date/Password:

Date/Password:

Date/Password:

Notes:

Website:

Email:

Username:

Date/Password:

Date/Password:

Date/Password:

Notes:

Website:

Email:

Username:

Date/Password:

Date/Password:

Date/Password:

Notes:

Website:

Email:

Username:

Date/Password:

Date/Password:

Date/Password:

Notes:

Website:

Email:

Username:

Date/Password:

Date/Password:

Date/Password:

Notes:

Website:

Email:

Username:

Date/Password:

Date/Password:

Date/Password:

Notes:

Website:
Email:
Username:
Date/Password:
Date/Password:
Date/Password:
Notes:

Website:
Email:
Username:
Date/Password:
Date/Password:
Date/Password:
Notes:

Website:
Email:
Username:
Date/Password:
Date/Password:
Date/Password:
Notes:

Website:

Email:

Username:

Date/Password:

Date/Password:

Date/Password:

Notes:

Website:

Email:

Username:

Date/Password:

Date/Password:

Date/Password:

Notes:

Website:

Email:

Username:

Date/Password:

Date/Password:

Date/Password:

Notes:

Website:

Email:

Username:

Date/Password:

Date/Password:

Date/Password:

Notes:

Website:

Email:

Username:

Date/Password:

Date/Password:

Date/Password:

Notes:

Website:

Email:

Username:

Date/Password:

Date/Password:

Date/Password:

Notes:

Website:

Email:

Username:

Date/Password:

Date/Password:

Date/Password:

Notes:

Website:

Email:

Username:

Date/Password:

Date/Password:

Date/Password:

Notes:

Website:

Email:

Username:

Date/Password:

Date/Password:

Date/Password:

Notes:

Website:

Email:

Username:

Date/Password:

Date/Password:

Date/Password:

Notes:

Website:

Email:

Username:

Date/Password:

Date/Password:

Date/Password:

Notes:

Website:

Email:

Username:

Date/Password:

Date/Password:

Date/Password:

Notes:

Website:

Email:

Username:

Date/Password:

Date/Password:

Date/Password:

Notes:

Website:

Email:

Username:

Date/Password:

Date/Password:

Date/Password:

Notes:

Website:

Email:

Username:

Date/Password:

Date/Password:

Date/Password:

Notes:

Website:

Email:

Username:

Date/Password:

Date/Password:

Date/Password:

Notes:

Website:

Email:

Username:

Date/Password:

Date/Password:

Date/Password:

Notes:

Website:

Email:

Username:

Date/Password:

Date/Password:

Date/Password:

Notes:

Website:

Email:

Username:

Date/Password:

Date/Password:

Date/Password:

Notes:

Website:

Email:

Username:

Date/Password:

Date/Password:

Date/Password:

Notes:

Website:

Email:

Username:

Date/Password:

Date/Password:

Date/Password:

Notes:

Website:

Email:

Username:

Date/Password:

Date/Password:

Date/Password:

Notes:

Website:

Email:

Username:

Date/Password:

Date/Password:

Date/Password:

Notes:

Website:

Email:

Username:

Date/Password:

Date/Password:

Date/Password:

Notes:

Website:

Email:

Username:

Date/Password:

Date/Password:

Date/Password:

Notes:

Website:

Email:

Username:

Date/Password:

Date/Password:

Date/Password:

Notes:

Website:

Email:

Username:

Date/Password:

Date/Password:

Date/Password:

Notes:

Website:
Email:
Username:
Date/Password:
Date/Password:
Date/Password:
Notes:

Website:
Email:
Username:
Date/Password:
Date/Password:
Date/Password:
Notes:

Website:
Email:
Username:
Date/Password:
Date/Password:
Date/Password:
Notes:

Website:_______________________________________

Email:____

Username:______________________________________

Date/Password:_________________________________

Date/Password:_________________________________

Date/Password:_________________________________

Notes:____

____

Website:_______________________________________

Email:____

Username:______________________________________

Date/Password:_________________________________

Date/Password:_________________________________

Date/Password:_________________________________

Notes:____

____

Q

Website:_______________________________________

Email:____

Username:______________________________________

Date/Password:_________________________________

Date/Password:_________________________________

Date/Password:_________________________________

Notes:____

____

Q

Website:

Email:

Username:

Date/Password:

Date/Password:

Date/Password:

Notes:

Website:

Email:

Username:

Date/Password:

Date/Password:

Date/Password:

Notes:

Website:

Email:

Username:

Date/Password:

Date/Password:

Date/Password:

Notes:

Website:

Email:

Username:

Date/Password:

Date/Password:

Date/Password:

Notes:

Website:

Email:

Username:

Date/Password:

Date/Password:

Date/Password:

Notes:

Website:

Email:

Username:

Date/Password:

Date/Password:

Date/Password:

Notes:

R

Website:

Email:

Username:

Date/Password:

Date/Password:

Date/Password:

Notes:

Website:

Email:

Username:

Date/Password:

Date/Password:

Date/Password:

Notes:

Website:

Email:

Username:

Date/Password:

Date/Password:

Date/Password:

Notes:

Website:

Email:

Username:

Date/Password:

Date/Password:

Date/Password:

Notes:

Website:

Email:

Username:

Date/Password:

Date/Password:

Date/Password:

Notes:

Website:

Email:

Username:

Date/Password:

Date/Password:

Date/Password:

Notes:

Website:

Email:

Username:

Date/Password:

Date/Password:

Date/Password:

Notes:

Website:

Email:

Username:

Date/Password:

Date/Password:

Date/Password:

Notes:

R

Website:

Email:

Username:

Date/Password:

Date/Password:

Date/Password:

Notes:

Website:

Email:

Username:

Date/Password:

Date/Password:

Date/Password:

Notes:

Website:

Email:

Username:

Date/Password:

Date/Password:

Date/Password:

Notes:

Website:

Email:

Username:

Date/Password:

Date/Password:

Date/Password:

Notes:

Website:____

Email:____

Username:____

Date/Password:_____________________________________

Date/Password:_____________________________________

Date/Password:_____________________________________

Notes:____

____

Website:____

Email:____

Username:____

Date/Password:_____________________________________

Date/Password:_____________________________________

Date/Password:_____________________________________

Notes:____

____

Website:____

Email:____

Username:____

Date/Password:_____________________________________

Date/Password:_____________________________________

Date/Password:_____________________________________

Notes:____

____

Website:

Email:

Username:

Date/Password:

Date/Password:

Date/Password:

Notes:

Website:

Email:

Username:

Date/Password:

Date/Password:

Date/Password:

Notes:

Website:

Email:

Username:

Date/Password:

Date/Password:

Date/Password:

Notes:

Website:

Email:

Username:

Date/Password:

Date/Password:

Date/Password:

Notes:

Website:

Email:

Username:

Date/Password:

Date/Password:

Date/Password:

Notes:

Website:

Email:

Username:

Date/Password:

Date/Password:

Date/Password:

Notes:

Website:

Email:

Username:

Date/Password:

Date/Password:

Date/Password:

Notes:

Website:

Email:

Username:

Date/Password:

Date/Password:

Date/Password:

Notes:

Website:

Email:

Username:

Date/Password:

Date/Password:

Date/Password:

Notes:

Website: ____

Email: ____

Username: ____

Date/Password: ____

Date/Password: ____

Date/Password: ____

Notes: ____

____

Website: ____

Email: ____

Username: ____

Date/Password: ____

Date/Password: ____

Date/Password: ____

Notes: ____

____

Website: ____

Email: ____

Username: ____

Date/Password: ____

Date/Password: ____

Date/Password: ____

Notes: ____

____

Website: _______________________________

Email: _______________________________

Username: _______________________________

Date/Password: _______________________________

Date/Password: _______________________________

Date/Password: _______________________________

Notes: _______________________________

____

Website: _______________________________

Email: _______________________________

Username: _______________________________

Date/Password: _______________________________

Date/Password: _______________________________

Date/Password: _______________________________

Notes: _______________________________

____

Website: _______________________________

Email: _______________________________

Username: _______________________________

Date/Password: _______________________________

Date/Password: _______________________________

Date/Password: _______________________________

Notes: _______________________________

____

Website:____

Email:____

Username:____

Date/Password:_____________________________________

Date/Password:_____________________________________

Date/Password:_____________________________________

Notes:____

____

Website:____

Email:____

Username:____

Date/Password:_____________________________________

Date/Password:_____________________________________

Date/Password:_____________________________________

Notes:____

____

Website:____

Email:____

Username:____

Date/Password:_____________________________________

Date/Password:_____________________________________

Date/Password:_____________________________________

Notes:____

____

Website:

Email:

Username:

Date/Password:

Date/Password:

Date/Password:

Notes:

Website:

Email:

Username:

Date/Password:

Date/Password:

Date/Password:

Notes:

Website:

Email:

Username:

Date/Password:

Date/Password:

Date/Password:

Notes:

Website:
Email:
Username:
Date/Password:
Date/Password:
Date/Password:
Notes:

Website:
Email:
Username:
Date/Password:
Date/Password:
Date/Password:
Notes:

Website:
Email:
Username:
Date/Password:
Date/Password:
Date/Password:
Notes:

Website: ____

Email: ____

Username: ____

Date/Password: ____

Date/Password: ____

Date/Password: ____

Notes: ____

____

Website: ____

Email: ____

Username: ____

Date/Password: ____

Date/Password: ____

Date/Password: ____

Notes: ____

____

Website: ____

Email: ____

Username: ____

Date/Password: ____

Date/Password: ____

Date/Password: ____

Notes: ____

____

U

Website: _______________________________

Email: _______________________________

Username: _______________________________

Date/Password: _______________________________

Date/Password: _______________________________

Date/Password: _______________________________

Notes: _______________________________

____

Website: _______________________________

Email: _______________________________

Username: _______________________________

Date/Password: _______________________________

Date/Password: _______________________________

Date/Password: _______________________________

Notes: _______________________________

____

Website: _______________________________

Email: _______________________________

Username: _______________________________

Date/Password: _______________________________

Date/Password: _______________________________

Date/Password: _______________________________

Notes: _______________________________

____

Website:

Email:

Username:

Date/Password:

Date/Password:

Date/Password:

Notes:

Website:

Email:

Username:

Date/Password:

Date/Password:

Date/Password:

Notes:

Website:

Email:

Username:

Date/Password:

Date/Password:

Date/Password:

Notes:

Website:

Email:

Username:

Date/Password:

Date/Password:

Date/Password:

Notes:

Website:

Email:

Username:

Date/Password:

Date/Password:

Date/Password:

Notes:

Website:

Email:

Username:

Date/Password:

Date/Password:

Date/Password:

Notes:

Website:

Email:

Username:

Date/Password:

Date/Password:

Date/Password:

Notes:

Website:

Email:

Username:

Date/Password:

Date/Password:

Date/Password:

Notes:

Website:

Email:

Username:

Date/Password:

Date/Password:

Date/Password:

Notes:

Website:

Email:

Username:

Date/Password:

Date/Password:

Date/Password:

Notes:

Website:

Email:

Username:

Date/Password:

Date/Password:

Date/Password:

Notes:

Website:

Email:

Username:

Date/Password:

Date/Password:

Date/Password:

Notes:

Website:

Email:

Username:

Date/Password:

Date/Password:

Date/Password:

Notes:

Website:

Email:

Username:

Date/Password:

Date/Password:

Date/Password:

Notes:

Website:

Email:

Username:

Date/Password:

Date/Password:

Date/Password:

Notes:

Website:

Email:

Username:

Date/Password:

Date/Password:

Date/Password:

Notes:

Website:

Email:

Username:

Date/Password:

Date/Password:

Date/Password:

Notes:

Website:

Email:

Username:

Date/Password:

Date/Password:

Date/Password:

Notes:

Website:

Email:

Username:

Date/Password:

Date/Password:

Date/Password:

Notes:

Website:

Email:

Username:

Date/Password:

Date/Password:

Date/Password:

Notes:

Website:

Email:

Username:

Date/Password:

Date/Password:

Date/Password:

Notes:

Website:

Email:

Username:

Date/Password:

Date/Password:

Date/Password:

Notes:

Website:

Email:

Username:

Date/Password:

Date/Password:

Date/Password:

Notes:

Website:

Email:

Username:

Date/Password:

Date/Password:

Date/Password:

Notes:

Website:

Email:

Username:

Date/Password:

Date/Password:

Date/Password:

Notes:

Website:

Email:

Username:

Date/Password:

Date/Password:

Date/Password:

Notes:

Website:

Email:

Username:

Date/Password:

Date/Password:

Date/Password:

Notes:

Website:

Email:

Username:

Date/Password:

Date/Password:

Date/Password:

Notes:

Website:

Email:

Username:

Date/Password:

Date/Password:

Date/Password:

Notes:

Website:

Email:

Username:

Date/Password:

Date/Password:

Date/Password:

Notes:

Website:

Email:

Username:

Date/Password:

Date/Password:

Date/Password:

Notes:

Website:

Email:

Username:

Date/Password:

Date/Password:

Date/Password:

Notes:

Website:

Email:

Username:

Date/Password:

Date/Password:

Date/Password:

Notes:

Website:

Email:

Username:

Date/Password:

Date/Password:

Date/Password:

Notes:

Website:

Email:

Username:

Date/Password:

Date/Password:

Date/Password:

Notes:

Website:

Email:

Username:

Date/Password:

Date/Password:

Date/Password:

Notes:

Website:

Email:

Username:

Date/Password:

Date/Password:

Date/Password:

Notes:

Website:

Email:

Username:

Date/Password:

Date/Password:

Date/Password:

Notes:

Website:

Email:

Username:

Date/Password:

Date/Password:

Date/Password:

Notes:

Website:

Email:

Username:

Date/Password:

Date/Password:

Date/Password:

Notes:

Website:

Email:

Username:

Date/Password:

Date/Password:

Date/Password:

Notes:

Website:

Email:

Username:

Date/Password:

Date/Password:

Date/Password:

Notes:

Website:

Email:

Username:

Date/Password:

Date/Password:

Date/Password:

Notes:

Website:

Email:

Username:

Date/Password:

Date/Password:

Date/Password:

Notes:

Website:

Email:

Username:

Date/Password:

Date/Password:

Date/Password:

Notes:

Y

Website:

Email:

Username:

Date/Password:

Date/Password:

Date/Password:

Notes:

Website:

Email:

Username:

Date/Password:

Date/Password:

Date/Password:

Notes:

Website:

Email:

Username:

Date/Password:

Date/Password:

Date/Password:

Notes:

Website:

Email:

Username:

Date/Password:

Date/Password:

Date/Password:

Notes:

Website:

Email:

Username:

Date/Password:

Date/Password:

Date/Password:

Notes:

Website:

Email:

Username:

Date/Password:

Date/Password:

Date/Password:

Notes:

Y

Website:

Email:

Username:

Date/Password:

Date/Password:

Date/Password:

Notes:

Website:

Email:

Username:

Date/Password:

Date/Password:

Date/Password:

Notes:

Website:

Email:

Username:

Date/Password:

Date/Password:

Date/Password:

Notes:

Website:

Email:

Username:

Date/Password:

Date/Password:

Date/Password:

Notes:

Website:

Email:

Username:

Date/Password:

Date/Password:

Date/Password:

Notes:

Website:

Email:

Username:

Date/Password:

Date/Password:

Date/Password:

Notes:

Website:_______________________________________

Email:____

Username:______________________________________

Date/Password:_________________________________

Date/Password:_________________________________

Date/Password:_________________________________

Notes:____

____

Website:_______________________________________

Email:____

Username:______________________________________

Date/Password:_________________________________

Date/Password:_________________________________

Date/Password:_________________________________

Notes:____

____

Website:_______________________________________

Email:____

Username:______________________________________

Date/Password:_________________________________

Date/Password:_________________________________

Date/Password:_________________________________

Notes:____

____

Website:

Email:

Username:

Date/Password:

Date/Password:

Date/Password:

Notes:

Website:

Email:

Username:

Date/Password:

Date/Password:

Date/Password:

Notes:

Website:

Email:

Username:

Date/Password:

Date/Password:

Date/Password:

Notes:

NOTES

NOTES

NOTES

Made in the USA
Monee, IL
07 July 2026